Winner of the Playwrights Theatre Centre's THE NEWS
Play Competition

Chosen as the University of Victoria's 2010/2011
Spotlight on Alumni project

"Anyone who has lost a parent or grandparent knows the
potential for drama—big and small—such is the simple
beauty of *The Josephine Knot*."
—*Monday Magazine*

"An endearing bit of emotional theatre."
—Bob Clark, *Calgary Herald*

THE JOSEPHINE KNOT

ALSO BY MEG BRAEM

Blood: A Scientific Romance

THE JOSEPHINE KNOT

MEG BRAEM

PLAYWRIGHTS CANADA PRESS
TORONTO

LIBRARY AND ARCHIVES CANADA CATALOGUING IN PUBLICATION
Braem, Meg, author
    The Josephine knot / Meg Braem. -- First edition.

A play.
Issued in print and electronic formats.
ISBN 978-1-77091-893-1 (softcover).--ISBN 978-1-77091-894-8 (PDF).
--ISBN 978-1-77091-895-5 (EPUB).--ISBN 978-1-77091-896-2 (Kindle)

    I. Title.

PS8603.R333J67 2018   C812'.6   C2017-907058-4
                                               C2017-907059-2

Playwrights Canada Press acknowledges that we operate on land which, for thousands of years, has been the traditional territories of the Mississaugas of the New Credit, the Huron-Wendat, the Anishinaabe, Métis, and the Haudenosaunee peoples. Today, this meeting place is still home to many Indigenous people from across Turtle Island and we are grateful to have the opportunity to work and play here.

We acknowledge the financial support of the Canada Council for the Arts—which last year invested $153 million to bring the arts to Canadians throughout the country—the Ontario Arts Council (OAC), the Ontario Media Development Corporation, and the Government of Canada for our publishing activities.

 Canada Council Conseil des arts
for the Arts   du Canada

 ONTARIO ARTS COUNCIL
CONSEIL DES ARTS DE L'ONTARIO
an Ontario government agency
un organisme du gouvernement de l'Ontario

 Canadä

 Ontario
Ontario Media Development
Corporation

For my father

FOREWORD

Being part of a family is hard. Writing about family is harder.

When we first started rehearsing the premiere production, a small group of us in an empty office that used to be the headquarters of the Victoria Fringe, Laura Harris, playing the role of Samantha, began the first read-through:

> Grandmothers will always die and their houses will always be pulled apart like meat from ribs. Hopping, squawking crows will always land to fight over every last morsel until all that's left is a mess of bone china and where you came from.

Such an evocative start. The immediacy of Grandma's death, the sense of poetic macabre, not to mention crows, which always make me think of Vancouver. We were obviously in the hands of a writer.

We went on to create two related productions of the show with our dedicated Bombus crew, one performed more immersively in the lobby of the Belfry Theatre, and the second back at our old school, the Phoenix at the University of Victoria. It is the mark of a good play that it was compelling in both versions, the text and storytelling shining forth. I still think of the Kaluke clan as many unique individuals, even though they were all performed by only the two actors, the vulnerable and generous Laura Harris and Brian Linds.

In an odd twist, a couple of years after the Belfry premiere I was about to direct a workshop of Meg's play *Blood*, and the day before, I was suddenly called away because my father was unconscious and in hospital. He died the day after I arrived. Much like Baba in *The Josephine Knot*, my father had spent his time gathering a bizarre collection of things, and I was now tasked to sort through them. A strange collection of books and papers and bags and Converse All Stars. I was living my own real-life version of the story and it brought into stark focus how real everything in this play is. It made me hear the "always" in the play in a different way. "Grandmothers will always die . . . " *Always*. Our loved ones will always die and families will always have to pick up the leftovers and make a home together. *Always*.

—Amiel Gladstone, 2018

Amiel Gladstone is a West Coast–based writer and director who has premiered work with companies such as Alberta Theatre Projects, the Arts Club Theatre Company, the Belfry Theatre, Caravan Farm Theatre, Factory Theatre, the Firehall Arts Centre, the Musical Stage Company, the National Arts Centre, Pacific Opera Victoria, Solo Collective, Vancouver Opera, Theatre Replacement, Theatre Conspiracy, Touchstone Theatre, Theatre SKAM, the Vancouver Playhouse, and the PuSh International Performing Arts Festival.

The Josephine Knot premiered at the Belfry Theatre in Victoria, BC, as part of Festival 08 and was produced by Theatre Bombus, with the following cast and crew:

David, and others: Brian Linds
Samantha, and others: Laura Harris

Director: Amiel Gladstone
Set and Costume Design: Megan Newton
Lighting Design: Jen Braem
Stage Manager: Sara Robb

The script was developed with the support of Caravan Farm Theatre and Playwrights Theatre Centre.

CHARACTERS

Samantha: Twenty-five
David: Sixty-five

Both actors weave in and out of playing the other characters that make
up the world of the play.

Auntie Babs: Played by the actor who is playing David.
Uncle Chris: Played by the actor who is playing David.
Vancouver Social Services: Played by the actor who is playing Samantha.
Betty Schooler: Played by the actor who is playing David.
Cousin Stephie: Played by the actor who is playing David.
Baba: Played by the actor who is playing Samantha.
Great Uncle Tommy: Played by the actor who is playing David.
Doctor: Played by the actor who is playing Samantha.
Robbie: Played by the actor who is playing David.

SETTING

Vancouver. Baba's wake. The wake is being held at her home with all of
her things being put out on display.

There is a large orange couch with a red-and-brown pattern splat-
tered all over it and an overstuffed chair with doilies on the back. There
is a coffee table, an end table, and a braided area rug. What seems like
thousands of jars of pickled items . . . eggs, cantaloupe, cucumbers,
watermelons, onions, herring, etc., are scattered around the space. The
jars are everywhere. They seem to be exploding out of the cupboards.
The house is cluttered with old keepsakes, brass ashtrays, an Expo '86
painting on velvet . . . that sort of thing.

SAMANTHA *addresses the audience while* DAVID, *her father, instructs the family members who have arrived for* BABA'*s wake.*

SAMANTHA   Grandmothers will always die and their houses will always be pulled apart like meat from ribs. Hopping, squawking crows will always land to fight over every last morsel until all that's left is a mess of bone china and where you came from.

DAVID   Here are the pens . . . please print clearly. You are welcome to put a label on something that already has a label. If this occurs, my brothers and I will discuss and decide what happens to said item. We will let that person know accordingly.

SAMANTHA   My grandmother's house has been opened up. We've cut her open to expose her organs. Relatives have crawled over highways to meet here. They descend upon the house with glinty eyes and a taste for blood.

DAVID   Please put your labels in a central spot where passersby are sure to see them.

SAMANTHA   The cupboards have been opened and there is a box of Sharpies and a roll of masking tape on the oak dining-room table. The guests are encouraged to write

their names on pieces of tape and label what they
might possibly want.

DAVID   If you are hungry, there are sandwiches, cheese plates,
                 pickles, and coffee on the oak table.

SAMANTHA   The matriarch has fallen and we scramble in the scraps.

DAVID   For those of you who don't drink coffee, there is a
                 bowl of punch in the kitchen, and Tim is putting on
                 a pot of tea.

SAMANTHA   Tim, Ted, Christopher, and David—my father and
                 also the eldest. She came here for a better life, at least
                 a better winter. She was pregnant with my father
                 when she left Alberta to come here. Four strong boys,
                 each born of a separate father. A mess of men born
                 out of another mess of men.

                 My grandmother has died.

DAVID   My mother has died.

SAMANTHA   Correction, my baba has died, as they would say back
                 on the farm. It is her womb and cheekbones that
                 thread the many paternal gene pools that make up
                 this family.

DAVID   It smells in here.

SAMANTHA   You can still smell beer and meat through the bleach
                 and rubbed-off glove rubber that my father and
                 uncles have scrubbed into the walls.

                 DAVID calls SAMANTHA into the world of the wake.

DAVID   A wake.

SAMANTHA   I am.

DAVID   No. A wake.

SAMANTHA   I am, Dad.

DAVID   No, Samantha. A . . . wake.

> *Shift.* DAVID *and* SAMANTHA *are both fully present in the world of the wake.*

Samantha, I want you to meet your auntie Babs.

> *The actor playing* DAVID *shifts physically into playing* BABS.

BABS   Well, aren't you the spitting image of Olga. Got her bones, didn't she, Dave?

SAMANTHA   *(to audience)* Auntie Babs is about three foot seven and all ass and perm. She's my dad's cousin from—

BABS   Back on the farm we could use a healthy girl like you.

SAMANTHA   I wonder how many times removed she is.

BABS   Apple doesn't fall from the tree, does it?

SAMANTHA   *(to audience)* I wonder about recessive genes.

BABS   And look at that hair . . . you got your grandmother's hair. Look at you! Is that hair real? Tell me that hair's not real.

SAMANTHA It is.

BABS Natural? Come here.

    She yanks on SAMANTHA's *hair.*

    You can't tell me that's natural.

SAMANTHA It is.

BABS You grew all that yourself?

SAMANTHA . . . I did.

BABS Well, my goodness. You know what it takes to get my hair like this?

    Beat.

    At least a hundred bucks every time I leave the salon . . . and that's not even counting the spray, which you can only buy at certain salons. It's the very best stuff.

SAMANTHA . . . I can tell.

BABS Spritzer to make it firm, mister to keep it . . . you know *(gestures to her hair being huge and high)*, oil to make it, well, oily—in a soft kind of way—and a gel that smells like mangoes. Is it mangoes? Maybe that other fruit, you know, the other one—

SAMANTHA Coconut?

BABS The other one, doesn't have a shell—

SAMANTHA   Banana.

BABS   No, no. Exotic. Costs a fortune at the Safeway and
             half the time its overripe—

SAMANTHA   Um, papaya?

BABS   Yes! That one! So pricey . . . you know when I was a
             kid we didn't have fruits like that. It was a real treat
             to get an orange in your Christmas stocking, but
             today . . . today we have to have it all; we have to
             have . . . what's it called?

SAMANTHA   Papaya.

BABS   Yes . . . those and . . . do you know how fattening avo-
             cados are? Who would have thought that a fruit . . .
             are they a fruit? They're green, which makes them
             seem like a vegetable, but tomatoes are a fruit . . . and
             you wouldn't think that, would you?

SAMANTHA   No.

BABS   Right . . . what was I saying?

SAMANTHA   I can't remember.

BABS   The gel! That's right. The gel, I use it to, you know, to
             make it . . .

SAMANTHA   Crunchy?

BABS   Defined.

BABS leans her head in front of SAMANTHA's nose.

Smell that.

SAMANTHA reluctantly takes a whiff.

The very best stuff.

BABS pulls out her spray, which resembles a spray-paint type bottle.

Course it's a pain in the summer with the fruit flies.

BABS begins to shellac her head.

SAMANTHA   *(to audience)* Dad's family. All the stories I've heard a hundred times . . .

The actor playing BABS shifts back to being DAVID.

DAVID   When I was in grade one we lived on the docks—

SAMANTHA   I know.

DAVID   We lived on the docks in a boat that your uncle Ted's father owned.

SAMANTHA   And it was slippery and you should never run on the docks. I know.

Beat.

I am so bored.

She relaxes and starts to fall asleep.

DAVID   Awake, Samantha!

SAMANTHA	That's what this is.
DAVID	Honey, you don't have to sit here and guard the Sharpies all night. Go on.
SAMANTHA	It's raining out.
DAVID	It's always raining in this city.

Shift. The song. The song is not musical but a ritual, a repeating of things that the family has said for years and years.

SAMANTHA	Vancouver.
DAVID	North are the mountains.
SAMANTHA	South are the ferries.

Flashback. DAVID *and* SAMANTHA *each come slowly from their separate sides of the stage.*

DAVID	WestJet.
SAMANTHA	Pacific Coach Line. Ferry walk-on.
DAVID	Visa.
SAMANTHA	Cash.
DAVID	Kelowna to Vancouver.
SAMANTHA	Island to Van, please.
DAVID	Could you make sure I get a receipt?

SAMANTHA   Are we allowed to eat on the bus?

DAVID   Can I get a drink?

SAMANTHA   There's no bathroom on the bus?

DAVID   I'll have a gin and tonic with a slice of lime.

SAMANTHA   Um, how long does the bus take to get on the ferry?

> *They meet in the middle. They look at each other and awkwardly hug.*

DAVID   How's school?

SAMANTHA   Done. How's work?

DAVID   Oh, you know . . . fine.

SAMANTHA   When do you retire?

DAVID   June.

SAMANTHA   Then what are you going to do?

DAVID   How's your mother?

SAMANTHA   Fine . . . she sends her condolences.

DAVID   Would you tell her thank you . . . for the card.

SAMANTHA   . . . sure.

> *They separate and become absorbed in their own worlds.*

DAVID   I hate this city.

SAMANTHA   Vancouver.

DAVID   Couldn't pay me to live in this city anymore.

SAMANTHA   The big city.

DAVID   So goddamn busy.

SAMANTHA   Standing in a crush of damp business suits on a greasy bus.

DAVID   The traffic so goddamn busy.

SAMANTHA   Steam rising like success off of expensive haircuts.

DAVID   Haven't spoken to anyone in this town for years.

SAMANTHA   Transfer to the SkyTrain. Smells like—

DAVID   (sniffing the air) Chinese pork, almond cakes.

SAMANTHA   I think my dad's best friend Chee-Lee lived around here.

DAVID   Wonder whatever happened to old Chee.

SAMANTHA   They met while studying mathematics at UBC.

DAVID   It's a different place now. When did it get so . . .

SAMANTHA   So fancy and well cut. So high in the heels and frothy and low in the fat. So shiny and bouncing in the bangs cut above perfectly arched eyebrows.

DAVID   But the rain's still there.

SAMANTHA   Wet streets littered with disintegrating latte cups.

DAVID   This old house rotting into the coast. The rain pound-
             ing down the roof like waves on a dock.

SAMANTHA   Dad always told me . . .

DAVID   Never run on the dock.

             Can't live on the coast anymore.

SAMANTHA   So absolutely gorgeous.

DAVID   Weather gives me headaches.

SAMANTHA   If you are thinking of a career you move here.

DAVID   Gets right into my sinuses.

SAMANTHA   Dad always told me I should go to UBC.

DAVID   Chee and I were in the same calculus class.

SAMANTHA   He also said I should become a doctor or at least a
             dentist.

DAVID   Maybe a surgeon, Sammy! I want you to think about
             becoming a surgeon.

SAMANTHA   And do what?

             Shift. We are back at the wake.

DAVID   Samantha . . . why don't you go and take a look
                 around? See if there's anything you want?

SAMANTHA   There's nothing here I want, Dad. It's just a bunch
                 of junk.

DAVID   Samantha Kaluke, this was your grandmother's house.
                 Go and pick out something to remember her by.

SAMANTHA   Cut her open, boys! What's that I see? Pass me a
                 scalpel, Tim. What is that, Ted? A lung? A bit of
                 spine? I think you know what we're going for here,
                 boys. Crack those ribs, Dave . . . I'm looking for the
                 heart.

DAVID   Samantha.

SAMANTHA   This isn't a wake. It's an autopsy.

DAVID   All you have to do is pick out something. Anything.

SAMANTHA   Fine.

                 SAMANTHA looks around without much commitment.

                 *DAVID shifts into Uncle CHRIS. He changes posture
                 and pops a chocolate into his mouth. Uncle CHRIS
                 is never found without a handful of chocolates in
                 his pockets.*

                 *SAMANTHA finds an old black-and-white photo.
                 Uncle CHRIS stands behind her.*

CHRIS   Looks different, eh?

SAMANTHA   Who is it?

CHRIS   Mum.

SAMANTHA   That's Baba?

CHRIS   Beautiful, eh? Always thought she could get a job doing advertisements.

SAMANTHA   Like model?

CHRIS   Why not? Mum was on her own with no money; I always thought she should model for chocolates. She had that dark hair. She was much richer and darker looking than all the blonds in the magazines. Perfect for double caramels and bonbons . . . plus I always figured she'd get free samples and we wouldn't have to go hungry.

SAMANTHA   Dad always told me, "You are what you eat."

CHRIS   Used to dream about eating chocolate pralines till our teeth fell out.

      He looks at the photo.

      Sure was a beauty all right.

      Shift. SAMANTHA *speaks to the audience.*

SAMANTHA   Why can't people die with dignity? Why did Elvis have to die on the toilet with his pants around his ankles and a bottle of half-digested pills fizzing out of his mouth?

Shift. Flashback. A phone rings. The actors shift to become new characters.

DAVID shifts into BETTY Schooler. SAMANTHA shifts to become SOCIAL SERVICES.

SOCIAL SERVICES *(recorded)* Hello and welcome to Vancouver Social Services. Our lines are currently busy. Your call is important to us. If you are calling as a witness to a domestic conflict, please press one. If you are calling as a victim of a domestic conflict, please press two. If you wish to return to the main menu, please press the pound key or stay on the line . . . a representative will be with you shortly.

Hold music . . . "The Girl From Ipanema."

Vancouver Social Services. How may I help you?

BETTY Yes. This is Betty Schooler on Pashdale Lane.

SOCIAL SERVICES How may I help you?

BETTY I'm calling about an odour.

SOCIAL SERVICES Ummm hmmm.

BETTY A smell coming from next door.

SOCIAL SERVICES What kind of smell, ma'am?

BETTY Well, kind of stomachy, like acid on meat and that sort of thing. Terribly really.

SOCIAL SERVICES Do you have any idea what it could be, ma'am?

BETTY   Yes, well actually. Actually, I was calling out of con-
                 cern for . . . well, I haven't seen Olga from next door
                 in about three weeks and well . . .

SOCIAL SERVICES Yes?

BETTY   She was at the grocery store . . . but I haven't seen her
                 since. There was a sale on chicken thighs.

SOCIAL SERVICES What are you trying to say, ma'am?

BETTY   I'm saying I think it might be her dead body that is
                 stinking up the neighbourhood.

                 Shift. Back to the wake.

SAMANTHA   How old is she in that picture?

                 CHRIS *flips it around and looks at the date.*

CHRIS   Judging by the date . . . about twenty-four or five . . .
                 how old are you, Sam?

SAMANTHA   Twenty-five.

CHRIS   About your age then . . . you got her looks, you know?
                 Same hair.

SAMANTHA   Dad says I got her temper.

CHRIS   God, she could knock the place down with a mood.
                 Good Lord. I'll never forget the time your dad locked
                 Ted, Tim, and me out in the front yard after our bath.
                 Mum found us out there, buck naked, pounding on
                 the door.

SAMANTHA   Dad did that?

CHRIS   We must have looked like three little piglets squealing
                    to come in.

SAMANTHA   He never told me that.

CHRIS   We got a whipping within an inch of our lives. Four
                    boys is a lot to handle for one mother.

SAMANTHA   Guess so.

CHRIS   You should put your tape on the picture, Samantha.

SAMANTHA   Maybe. I'm going to look around first.

CHRIS   You can put your name on more than one thing,
                    you know?

SAMANTHA   I know, but Dad told me to look around. I think I'll
                    know what I want when I see it.

CHRIS   Suit yourself, kiddo. I'm famished. You want a
                    sandwich?

SAMANTHA   No thanks, Uncle Chris.

CHRIS   Those pastrami and Swiss ones aren't too bad.

SAMANTHA   Maybe a pickle.

CHRIS   Suit yourself, kiddo.

SAMANTHA *looks over the assortment of Safeway cheese platters, premade sandwiches, and vegetable trays.*

SAMANTHA (*to audience*) I know they came from a store but I cannot break the oath that I would never eat another meal in this house.

Shift.

DAVID Eat up.

SAMANTHA When I was eight, my dad brought me down to visit my grandmother and also promised me a visit to the Vancouver Aquarium.

SAMANTHA *shifts into her child self.*

DAVID I said eat up, kiddo.

SAMANTHA Dad, what is this?

DAVID It's shepherd's pie. Eat up and we can go see Shamu.

SAMANTHA Shamu is in Florida, Dad. It's Bjossa here.

DAVID Well, do you want to see the whales or not? Eat your lunch.

SAMANTHA (*whispers*) Dad?

DAVID What?

SAMANTHA I saw something fly into the dish.

DAVID   What?

SAMANTHA   I did. I saw a fly land and go under the tinfoil covering
             the dish.

DAVID   Samantha, I mean it. Eat up or we won't go to the
             aquarium.

SAMANTHA   No, Dad, I'm serious. Look, there's another one.

             They watch a fly go into the dish.

DAVID   Well, I'll be damned.

SAMANTHA   Look, Dad! See the flies?

             *DAVID goes over to the cast-iron bake pan and lifts
             the tinfoil. The two of them jump back as they see
             the dish is crawling with maggots.*

             Ewwww! Gross!

DAVID   Jesus Christ!

SAMANTHA   What are all those little white things, Dad?

DAVID   Maggots!

SAMANTHA   Maggots?

DAVID   Those are the larva of houseflies!

SAMANTHA   What's a larva?

DAVID

Those are all going to be houseflies. They're nesting in the shepherd's pie.

SAMANTHA makes a face and turns to throw up.

Let's go, sweetie. I'll buy you a burger on the way to see the whales.

SAMANTHA shifts into her adult self again.

SAMANTHA

(to audience) And from then on we ate at the White Spot when we were visiting. Dad said Baba had always been like that, crap on the counters. I'd keep the cardboard ships from my Pirate Pak meals in the car and have sea battles on the drive back to the interior. Over the next few years, our visits became less and less frequent, stopping altogether when I was about thirteen.

Three years after we saw Bjossa in Vancouver, Tilikum, a whale in Victoria, accidentally killed a trainer when she slipped on the deck and fell into the tank. He thought she did it to play and pulled her down into the water for a game of tag. Her lungs filled with water and they fished her body out twenty minutes later when he found her unsportsmanlike in her lack of enthusiasm.

DAVID begins to open jars of preserves to be put out on the table.

They've cracked open her pickle jars. She pickled everything she could in those huge jars.

The following is said at the same time. DAVID is heard at a lower level than SAMANTHA.

They look like cucumber fish tanks when you stick your eye up to the glass. Lake weeds of dill with big fat cucumbers lumbering by, laying their dill-seed eggs—

DAVID

Pickled herring, not traditional, but we love it. You can eat the pickles, Sam. Those cucumbers have sat in vinegar for so long nothing could ever survive in that glass. Eat up!

SAMANTHA

But Dad! The worms!

DAVID

It's good for you.

SAMANTHA

So that's why I never eat anything in my baba's house that isn't pickled.

DAVID

Pickled cantaloupe?

SAMANTHA

And I never eat the pickled cantaloupe that she sent for Christmas every year.

DAVID

Eat up, Samantha!

SAMANTHA

(to audience) Bio eleven. My teacher, Mr. Potsworth, brings out a key and lets us in the room behind the slide projector. Inside there are walls and walls of jars. Inside each jar there is something floating. Specimens. A baby shark . . . no, a premature dog-fish . . . a fetal pig . . . One jar has a silt of sloughed-off tissue sitting in a layer at the bottom. When the teacher lifts it, the tissue floats up and the jar clouds like a Christmas snow globe. We walk to the back of the room and he pries open the seal of a huge white bucket. As he lifts the lid, there is a terrible

smell. Formaldehyde—keeps them forever. Inside are twenty-four calves' eyeballs with silky membranes hanging off them. It looks like a gigantic bowl of won ton soup.

DAVID

Eat up, Samantha.

SAMANTHA

I don't know why we buried her. She could have been jarred and set out on the oak table with the Safeway meats and gherkins. Floating by with a green smile on her face while we picked over her stuff. Keep her forever.

Shift. DAVID *reads from a list.*

DAVID

A bone china teacup with a burgundy pattern laced in gold plate sitting in its perfect saucer; a little Hawaiian girl laughing in the rain painted on black velvet; a blown glass ashtray that looks like an abstract sea anemone; sandpaper stickers shaped like daisies on the bottom of the pink tub to keep you from slipping; angelfish making kissy faces on the bathroom wall; an ancient record player; and sitting on the hearth, a pair of—

DAVID *transforms into* COUSIN STEPHIE, *who is twenty-six years old.* SAMANTHA *and* COUSIN STE-PHIE *exclaim in unison:*

PLASTIC DEER!

COUSIN STEPHIE

Do you want them?

SAMANTHA

Who are you?

COUSIN STEPHIE   Who are you?

SAMANTHA   I'm David's daughter. This is my grandmother's
                   house.

COUSIN STEPHIE   I'm your dad's cousin . . . Stephie.

SAMANTHA   My dad never told me about you.

COUSIN STEPHIE   Well, technically I'm your dad's cousin's daughter.

SAMANTHA   Really? I've never heard your name—

COUSIN STEPHIE   Oh, we're removed and our sides of the family don't
                   talk much.

SAMANTHA   What's on your list?

COUSIN STEPHIE   Some crystal, some china . . . the grandfather clock.

SAMANTHA   I thought your side didn't really talk to my side?

COUSIN STEPHIE   We don't.

SAMANTHA   Then why do you want all that stuff if you don't really
                   care about her?

COUSIN STEPHIE   Oh, we care deeply! We were just busy. It's a very long
                   way to come, a very long way.

SAMANTHA   (under her breath) And because you think that crystal
                   is real.

COUSIN STEPHIE   Pardon?

SAMANTHA   Nothing.

COUSIN STEPHIE   Do you want them?

SAMANTHA   The plastic deer?

COUSIN STEPHIE   Yes, do you want them, because they would look darling next to my Robbie's rhododendron.

SAMANTHA   Robbie?

COUSIN STEPHIE   Robbie? My boyfriend. My fiancé. We're going to get engaged soon. Do you want them?

SAMANTHA   I . . .

COUSIN STEPHIE   Do you want them because we're going to get engaged, us. We're going to and then I'm going to move in and they would look great next to the rhododendron in the front yard . . . so do you?

SAMANTHA   Yes, I do. I want one.

COUSIN STEPHIE   Well, it's a set, so if you want them you have to take them both.

SAMANTHA   Both? I can probably only fit one of them in my apartment.

COUSIN STEPHIE   Well, maybe you don't want them.

SAMANTHA   I played with them when I was little. I made us be very still so the hunter couldn't see us. I love their glass eyes that glow orange.

COUSIN STEPHIE   Well decide, because if you don't take them I will.

SAMANTHA   I don't know . . .

COUSIN STEPHIE   We're hoping to be on the highway by six.

SAMANTHA   Ahh, maybe you should have them if I can't decide.

COUSIN STEPHIE   Done. Thank you . . .

                  (to herself) I'll saw off the tops and plant begonias
                  inside.

                  *COUSIN STEPHIE takes out a pen and starts to make
                  a label with her name on it. SAMANTHA notices
                  something.*

SAMANTHA   Hey! What's that?

COUSIN STEPHIE   What?

SAMANTHA   On the back of your shirt? Is that a label?

COUSIN STEPHIE   No.

                  *COUSIN STEPHIE tries desperately to reach the label
                  stuck to her back.*

SAMANTHA   Yes, it is. What does that say? (reading the name on
                  the label) TIM. Are you taking people's names off of
                  things?

COUSIN STEPHIE   NO . . . (under her breath) Must be from the grand-
                  father clock.

SAMANTHA   You're stealing stuff that people care about!

COUSIN STEPHIE   Fine. You can have the plastic deer!

SAMANTHA   No, I don't want them! I want them in your yard,
                  where their orange glass eyes will remind you of what
                  you've done. You take them and let your Bobby's
                  gladiolas rot all over them.

COUSIN STEPHIE   ROBBIE! As in the Rob part of Robert . . . It's not like
                  they're worth anything.

SAMANTHA   I know that.

COUSIN STEPHIE   They're crap. This whole house is full of crap.

SAMANTHA   I know, but I remember them.

COUSIN STEPHIE   Well, I can use them.

                  She turns to leave.

                  So much crap I can barely move in here.

                  Shift.

SAMANTHA   *(to audience)* When my dad and uncles got here they
                  could smell the house from up the street. No one
                  answered the door so they had to break it down.
                  They could barely get the thing open because there
                  were years and years of newspapers stacked in the
                  hallway. The smell was enough to make you want
                  to puke.

DAVID   And your uncle Chris did.

SAMANTHA	There was food all over the counter and beer cans piled in every room. My dad and his brothers looked around quietly, expecting to stumble upon a corpse. Only . . .
DAVID	She wasn't dead.
SAMANTHA	Finally, they find this tiny woman. I mean they didn't even recognize her at first. The weight of the grease had pulled her hair straight and she stunk like sweat. She was huddled in the bathtub with a blanket, a pillow, and a back scrubber. She'd obviously been sleeping in there since her bed was so covered in newspapers, magazines, and mouse droppings that she couldn't get into it.

Shift. SAMANTHA *turns into* BABA.

DAVID	Mum?
BABA	What?
DAVID	Mum, is that you?
BABA	. . . David? David, is that you?
DAVID	Yes, Mum. We're going to take you somewhere safe, okay?
BABA	I don't want to go, David. Tell them I'm fine. Tell them to get out of my house. I don't want strangers in my house.
DAVID	They're not strangers, Mum. I'm here with Chris, Tim, and Ted—your sons.

BABA   David, when you were young we lived on the docks.

DAVID   I know, Mum.

BABA   In a boat tied to the docks—that Teddy's father owned.

DAVID   Mum, when was the last time you took a bath?

BABA   Every night, David. I take a bath every night.

DAVID   No, Mum, you're sleeping in the bath. You're sleeping in the bath, not washing in there. When was the last time you took a bath with water?

BABA   David?

DAVID   Yes, Mum.

BABA   You aren't going to make me go, are you?

Shift. SAMANTHA *is herself.*

SAMANTHA   He took her to the hospital while my uncles went to the grocery store to get cleaning supplies.

Shift. DAVID *turns into Great* UNCLE TOMMY.

UNCLE TOMMY   Is that you, Samantha?

SAMANTHA *turns around.*

SAMANTHA   Yes?

UNCLE TOMMY   It's me, your great uncle Tommy.

SAMANTHA   Oh, Uncle Tommy. I didn't recognize you.

UNCLE TOMMY   *(lifts sleeves)* Recognize these?

SAMANTHA   Your tattoos! I remember wishing my dad had been born with anchors on his forearms.

UNCLE TOMMY   Born with?

SAMANTHA   That's what I thought when I was little.

UNCLE TOMMY   A life on the fish boats and a good piss up are what these are born of . . . mostly a good piss up. God you're big, all grown up.

SAMANTHA   Yeah, I guess so.

UNCLE TOMMY   How old does that make your dad now?

SAMANTHA   Sixty-five. Retiring this year.

UNCLE TOMMY   I'll be damned, retiring. Here I am, nothing but a briny old sailor and your dad's retiring.

SAMANTHA   He'll have been with the company six months short of thirty years. I don't think he really knows what to do with himself.

UNCLE TOMMY   Happens to the best of us. I'm still trying to get my land legs. Goddamn, so he's stepping out of the world, eh? I guess that means you're stepping in then?

SAMANTHA   I guess so.

UNCLE TOMMY   You're the new us. It's you representing us now, Samantha. How's that feel?

SAMANTHA   Fine, I think.

UNCLE TOMMY   When your dad was in grade one, they lived on the docks.

SAMANTHA   I know.

UNCLE TOMMY   In Coal Harbour, they lived on the boat that Ted's father owned.

SAMANTHA   You don't say.

UNCLE TOMMY   Olga didn't have two pennies to rub together. I was still just a kid back on the farm. Only place she had to sleep was on that boat. Take a good look around, 'cause this is where you come from. This is what you're bringing into the world.

SAMANTHA   Dear God.

UNCLE TOMMY   So what are you going to do? How are you going to make us proud?

                Shift. UNCLE TOMMY *shifts back into* DAVID.

SAMANTHA
& DAVID   Thirty-seven garbage bags of shit.

DAVID   Old papers and napkins. An entire closet filled with those little ketchup and mustard packs she must have been picking up at food courts. An entire freezer full of meat that had been rotting since BC Hydro turned off the electricity: Thanksgiving turkeys, rib-eye steaks, pork cutlets that had dried out from freezer burn. The smell—that's probably what they thought was her. That rotting meat probably saved her life. God knows how long this would have gone on if the neighbours hadn't called.

Shift. SAMANTHA *becomes the* DOCTOR.

DOCTOR   Gangrene.

DAVID   What?

DOCTOR   Your mother has gangrene in her left leg. Looks like she got a cut and it somehow got infected.

DAVID   It's that damned house. The whole place was probably crawling with bacteria.

DOCTOR   We're going to have to take it off.

DAVID   You're going to amputate?

DOCTOR   If we'd gotten to it a couple of weeks ago she might have had a chance, but as it is there is nothing we can do.

DAVID   Goddamn, I hate it here.

Shift. The song repeats. SAMANTHA *is herself.*

SAMANTHA   North are the mountains.

DAVID   South are the ferries.

SAMANTHA   If you are seriously looking for a career you move here—

DAVID   A surgeon, Sammy! What do you think about the idea of becoming a surgeon?

SAMANTHA   I could cut people for a living.

DAVID   How does that sound? You could be a surgeon and save people's lives.

SAMANTHA   *(to audience)* They did it. They cut it, but when my dad and I went in to see her it looked like they'd cut off more than just her leg. She was so small. Her weight under the blankets looked more like a bundled towel than a body. Her face seemed changed and there seemed to be no weight to hold her down to this world.

            Shift. The hospital. SAMANTHA *covers herself with a blanket to become* BABA.

BABA   David? David? Where am I?

DAVID   You're in the hospital, Mum. You're in the hospital and I'm here with Samantha.

BABA   Samantha?

DAVID   She's right here, Mum. We've come to see you and bring you some flowers.

            SAMANTHA *stands to become herself. She bundles the blanket and puts it where she was prior to standing.*

They speak to the blanket bundle. SAMANTHA *picks up a cone of paper representing a bouquet.*

SAMANTHA   Yeah, Baba. I'm right here. Look.

She shows her the flowers.

DAVID   Irises, your favourite.

SAMANTHA   Look how dark and purple they are. Look how nice they make the room.

DAVID   Samantha picked these out especially for you, Mum.

DAVID goes to show BABA the flowers. As he does this, the paper uncoils and a pile of Popsicle sticks spill out. Shift. We are at the wake.

Dammit.

SAMANTHA   What happened?

DAVID   I just tried to turn it on and it fell apart.

SAMANTHA   What is it?

DAVID gathers the Popsicle sticks.

DAVID   I made it in grade five. It was a lamp. See? This is part of the shade and then the light bulb stuck in here, and this made the base and then it kind of stood up like this . . .

SAMANTHA   You made that?

DAVID

I just wanted to see if it still worked. The glue must have begun to dissolve. There were over three hundred Popsicle sticks in this thing.

SAMANTHA

Wow.

DAVID

Yeah . . . wow.

Beat. DAVID *examines one of the ancient Popsicle sticks.*

It was a Mother's Day gift.

They pick the sticks up off the ground.

Once we sat in a movie theatre for the whole day to get out of the rain.

SAMANTHA

Can I have one?

DAVID

One what?

SAMANTHA

Can I have one of the Popsicle sticks?

DAVID

Sure. It's trash now I suppose.

SAMANTHA *puts the Popsicle stick in her pocket and turns around to step into the bathroom. She picks up a hand-held mirror and looks at herself in it. The shower curtain is pulled back and we see* ROBBIE *(played by* DAVID*) smoking a joint.*

ROBBIE

Oh, hey.

SAMANTHA

I-I didn't know there was anyone in here.

ROBBIE   Yeah, I figured I should let you know I'm in here
             before you sit on the can or something.

SAMANTHA   Uh, are we related?

ROBBIE   Probably not. I'm Robbie.

SAMANTHA   Robbie? Oh, Robbie. I met your fiancée earlier.

ROBBIE   Girlfriend.

SAMANTHA   Oh.

ROBBIE   Care for a hit?

SAMANTHA   Are you hotboxing my baba's shower?

ROBBIE   Guess so.

SAMANTHA   Can't you do this outside?

ROBBIE   It's raining outside.

SAMANTHA   It's always raining in this city.

ROBBIE   Yeah? You from here?

SAMANTHA   No, I live on the island.

ROBBIE   What island?

SAMANTHA   Vancouver Island.

ROBBIE   I thought you said you weren't from Vancouver.

SAMANTHA   I'm not. I live in Victor— Look, just forget it.

ROBBIE   They got good weed here, eh?

SAMANTHA   They do.

ROBBIE   Why don't you join me?

SAMANTHA   I don't think so.

ROBBIE   Come on, take the stress off.

SAMANTHA   . . . It's been a long day.

> She steps into the bathtub to join him. She takes the joint, has a pull.

ROBBIE   What's that sound?

SAMANTHA   It's the rain on the roof.

ROBBIE   Oh.

> He inhales another pull.

You want some more?

> SAMANTHA reaches her hand out. He leans in, exhales in her mouth, and kisses her. She pushes him away.

SAMANTHA   What are you doing?

ROBBIE   What?

SAMANTHA   We're practically related. My sort of cousin is your fiancée!

ROBBIE   Girlfriend!

SAMANTHA leaves.

God, this family.

SAMANTHA   *(to audience)* My mum hasn't seen Baba since that trip to the aquarium. She and my dad got a divorce, sold the house, and we moved to the island. Dad stayed in the interior, bought a brand new pink house. Baba always said it was an ugly pink house. Wouldn't let him forget it.

Pickling her whole body, maybe that wasn't the way to go, might've deterred the greed. Maybe just a shrine, a coffee table in the centre of her living room with one of her jars on it. We could each walk by and pay our respects to the leg floating in a nest of dill.

Shift. The hospital.

BABA   David?

DAVID   Mum?

BABA   What happened?

DAVID   You fell because there was so much stuff piled around and you couldn't move very easily.

BABA   Move? Who has moved?

DAVID
: You cut yourself and the house infected it. Your leg was amputated, Mum.

SAMANTHA
: I don't think she can hear you. I think she's gone back to sleep.

DAVID
: Oh . . . Good night, Mum.

SAMANTHA
: *(to audience)* She died three weeks later. She fell while trying to crawl under her bed and drink the can of beer Uncle Ted had snuck in to her. I don't think she realized she only had one leg. They found her with an orange blanket twisted around her stump and bruises on her cheek where she'd cracked her face. She was lying in a pool of Pilsner, which was slowly being absorbed into the paper of her gown. I think she must have looked kind of pretty. The blood had burst the tiny capillaries of her face, giving her the look of a blushing bride.

> *Shift. Back at the wake.* DAVID *waves one of the rolls of tape around so the mourners can see.*

DAVID
: More tape? Please take a roll. I want to get rid of as much as I can, makes it easier.

SAMANTHA
: Easier?

DAVID
: To deal with the house.

SAMANTHA
: What about the house?

DAVID
: When we sell it.

SAMANTHA
: What?

DAVID	We're selling it, Samantha. There's nothing here worth anything. It'll all be picked over by the end of the day and then we're selling it.
SAMANTHA	What do you mean when *we're* selling it?
DAVID	I'm selling it. It's nothing but a pile of rot. The roof needs to be replaced. I don't think we'll ever be able to get all that meat smell out.
SAMANTHA	You don't make these decisions, Dad.
DAVID	I already did.
SAMANTHA	You can't just . . . what did Uncle Tim say? Uncle Ted?
DAVID	Someone has to make the decisions.
SAMANTHA	You have to talk to your brothers.
DAVID	What are we going to do, Sam? Cut it up four ways? It's not a cake. The thing to do is to sell it—the whole property—the whole shebang, and we'll split the money. Some developer can buy it and build something new.
SAMANTHA	But this is Baba's house.
DAVID	She's gone, Sammy.
SAMANTHA	I know that, Dad. I know . . . but this was the house. This is where the family was.
DAVID	Samantha, you haven't been here in years.

SAMANTHA   So? It was here. This is where we would come to be together, Christmas and summertimes. If it's gone then there is nothing to tie us together. There's nowhere to meet.

DAVID   Samantha, you're an adult now. You should understand. It makes the most sense to sell.

SAMANTHA   Dad, this isn't your decision to make.

DAVID   Well, it isn't yours.

SAMANTHA   No, but it isn't yours. The whole family needs to get together to talk this out.

DAVID   Fine, let's talk it out right now!

SAMANTHA   For God sake's, Dad, can't you wait until today is over?

DAVID   Why? Isn't this why we're here? Get a pen and a piece of tape and write the words "For Sale" on the front door.

SAMANTHA   I'm getting Uncle Ted.

DAVID   Leave it alone, Samantha.

SAMANTHA   Leave it alone? Jesus, Dad, look what happened the last time you did that?

            Beat.

            Why didn't you check on her?

DAVID   I did. I called every once in a while. She always
             seemed fine.

SAMANTHA   How the hell could she have seemed fine? Her leg was
             rotting. Why'd you let the house rot and kill her?

DAVID   Look, I did what I could, all right? We don't live here.
             I didn't know.

SAMANTHA   But, Dad, you just left her alone and she rotted in her
             huge piles of her past and her shit. How come you
             weren't there?

DAVID   Samantha, look, sometimes you have to leave your
             family to start your own.

SAMANTHA   But you left the family; you started your own family
             and you left us too!

DAVID   Samantha, I never—

SAMANTHA   Yes, Dad, you did. It's your fault that we're here with
             all this crap, because she doesn't have to be dead and
             you just want to get rid of it all . . . the whole family,
             pretend it never happened.

                  Beat.

DAVID   Samantha . . . when I was in grade one we lived on
             the docks.

SAMANTHA   I KNOW THAT!

DAVID   We lived on the docks in the boat that your uncle
             Ted's father owned.

SAMANTHA	I already know this story.
DAVID	His name was Len and he drank a lot.
SAMANTHA	And they were always fighting.
DAVID	The others weren't born yet and your uncle Ted was in a crib warming by the stove.
SAMANTHA	If you tell me never to—
DAVID	Your baba was cooking dinner and he came in. He grabbed her like that a lot. Tried to pull her away from the stove and onto the bed. It happened so fast. She was tired, she was hurt, and she'd had enough. She hit him right on the top of the face. The sweet red crack of a cast-iron frying pan, and in that one second there was blood everywhere, all over the placemats, all over the stove, the floor, Teddy's crib, and her face . . .
SAMANTHA	Dad?
DAVID	I turned and ran. I ran as fast as I could. I didn't know where I was going but I wasn't coming back. The wood was wet with the rain and I tripped and fell over the edge of the dock. Sploosh.
SAMANTHA	*(whispers to herself)* Never run on the dock.
DAVID	I couldn't swim and I beat my arms and screamed water down my throat. It was like a pool of rain to wash the blood away. Suddenly, a hand grabbed my shirt and pulled me onto the dock. It was her. She held me so tight that she was soaked through. My

ribs stung from pressure and water. It was so tight I felt like the ropes, twisted up and dangling in the water. Two lines tied to make one. A perfect knot . . .

Beat.

(gestures to the mess) I never meant for all this shit to happen.

SAMANTHA   She was old, Dad.

DAVID   Yeah, she had lived a long time.

> DAVID *collapses in an old easy chair.*

SAMANTHA   *(to audience)* I go upstairs into the guest room. Inside, I sit with the piles of wilting books that have been tied together with twine. Quiet, just a few moments of quiet. I find a book on sailing. I look through and think about Uncle Tommy's fishing stories.

UNCLE TOMMY   Never piss into the wind, Samantha.

> SAMANTHA *searches through the book.*

SAMANTHA   Monkey's fist, bowline, reef, and I find it . . . the Josephine knot. A knot for making two lines one. I untie a piece of twine from a pile of books and begin to wind it up. I think about how my father must be missing his mother.

DAVID   Once, when we had no money, we shared a box of peppermints for dinner.

> SAMANTHA *ties the two ends of the line together.*

SAMANTHA   The perfect knot.

              *She pulls the Popsicle stick out of her pocket and
              looks at it. She stuffs the twine and Popsicle stick
              back in her pocket and gets up to find her dad sort-
              ing through junk while referring to a small notepad.*

DAVID   One for the copper jelly moulds, seven for the oak
              dining-room table, five for the half set of crystal
              glasses . . .

SAMANTHA   *(to audience)* You can hear it. You can hear it over
              the fights for the Royal Doulton gravy boat. There's
              a silence. She's left a space.

              DAVID *fidgets with an ancient record player to see if
              it still works. A song begins to play, a song he hasn't
              heard in a very long time.* SAMANTHA *watches him
              for a moment before entering enough to make him
              aware of her presence.*

DAVID   Honey, did you look around?

SAMANTHA   Yeah.

DAVID   I found your auntie Babs bringing stuff in. I thought
              she was taking things before we discussed it but she
              was actually bringing in a box of her own broken
              teacups, a chipped teapot, and melted Tupperware. I
              guess she was hoping some poor griever would take
              it home.

SAMANTHA   Baba never used Tupperware. She wasn't one for put-
              ting things away.

DAVID   Did you find anything you wanted?

SAMANTHA   *(to audience)* If I could have anything I would have my baba's pickled leg. I would even like to see the part that they cut. I'd like to see where all the veins wrapped up into the rest of her. Making two parts one.

(to DAVID) Not really. Not any more than anyone else.

(to audience) I would take the jar and bury it in the backyard.

DAVID   Well all right, but if you change your mind come get this roll of tape. I'm going to get something to eat. You want something?

DAVID sorts through the jars to find cucumber pickles.

SAMANTHA   Okay.

DAVID opens the jar. They each eat a pickle.

DAVID   She sure made 'em good.

SAMANTHA   Sure did.

DAVID   *(sighs)* It's been a long day.

SAMANTHA   How about a bit of fresh air? Get out of the house?

DAVID   I'm sure I could leave for a minute.

SAMANTHA puts her fingers in the jar and gets an idea. She grabs the pickle jar and brings it with her.

They go out to the front yard. SAMANTHA *takes out a pickle and kneels down.*

SAMANTHA Okay, Dad, take a bite. You are what you eat. The house ate Baba. We eat these. Make two things one.

SAMANTHA holds the pickle up for her father to take a bite. She follows with her own bite into the pickle. She lays the pickle into the earth. She pulls the Popsicle stick from her pocket and breaks it in half. She reaches back into her pocket to pull out the twine. She wraps the Popsicle stick with the twine, fashioning a cross. She places it at the head of the pickle's grave. She reaches up to get her father to kneel with her.

Do you have anything you want to say?

DAVID I don't know.

SAMANTHA Anything, Dad.

DAVID I don't know, Samantha. We're sitting in the dirt eating a dead woman's canning.

SAMANTHA I'll go first. Goodbye, Baba, um, you had a long life. I don't know, maybe you were ready for it. Maybe you stayed in the house because you knew what was happening. I don't know. I know that you make the best pickles, with the most dill, and they always stay crunchy and now *(takes a bite out of a pickle)* you and the house will always be with us . . . uh . . . okay, Dad, your turn.

Beat.

Anything.

DAVID   I'll always remember you, Mum . . . That night, walking home from the movie theatre in the rain, eating a box of peppermints. You stopped at the edge of the dock and just stared at the water. I'll never forget it.

Beat.

SAMANTHA   What was she doing?

DAVID   Trying to make a decision.

SAMANTHA   What kind of decision?

DAVID   Whether or not to jump.

Beat.

We didn't have anywhere else to go.

I stood beside her and watched her face. I thought she was going to leave me there by myself, in the rain.

SAMANTHA   You never told me that.

DAVID   She finally looked up; she took my hand and we walked away from the water. We got my brother and never went back to the boat Ted's father owned again. She got a job as a seamstress, met Christopher's father, and eventually bought this house.

DAVID looks to the pickle grave.

I miss you, Mum, and I'm sorry for how things ended up. Thank you for everything you ever did.

Beat.

Samantha, you know I only ever wanted the best for you.

SAMANTHA   Yeah, Dad, I know.

(to audience) I think about my dad and everything he ever told me.

DAVID   You should never hike while menstruating, Samantha. The bears can smell it.

SAMANTHA   Grandmothers will always die and their houses will always be pulled apart until all that's left is a mess of bone china, hearts, and what you are a part of. I think about my dad and everything he ever told me.

DAVID   *(SAMANTHA whispers with him)* The colours of family are the same ones that show up in bruises. There's the deep purple of gasoline on water, the dark blues of the dock on rainy nights—

(said by DAVID alone) —and the pale yellow of the light that's been left on for you to find your way home.

She passes a pickle to her dad and takes one for herself. They clink them together and eat. Lights fade to the sound of crunchy pickles and a light rain.

The end.

ACKNOWLEDGEMENTS

I would like to thank Heidi Taylor at Playwrights Theatre Centre, who was my first dramaturg and was so supportive and helpful. Thank you to Estelle Shook, who hosted me at Caravan Farm during the writing of this play. I would also like to thank Ami Gladstone, who first read an early draft at the farm and was indispensable along the way. With Ami at the helm, Brian Linds and Laura Harris on stage, Meg Newton's plethora of pickles lit by Jen Braem, and Sara Robb managing it all, I couldn't be more thankful for this team. Thank you to Theatre Bombus. I think of our time together with that scrappy little theatre company with the fondest of memories. Thank you to Roy Surette, who after hearing this drizzly little play read on a sunny afternoon saw that it had a home. Thank you to Vern Thiessen, who compelled me to remember this story, and to Annie Gibson and Blake Sproule at Playwrights Canada Press for helping me share it. Thank you to my family, who, over pots of coffee, see that no one is forgotten and no story is left untold. Thank you to my baba, whose strength I hope lives on in the rest of us. Most profoundly, thank you to my father, Trevor Braem, whose abundance of humour, heart, and sometimes temper was an unbreakable thread tying us together. I miss you.

Meg Braem's plays have won the Gwen Pharis Ringwood Award for Drama at the Alberta Literary Awards and the Alberta Playwriting Competition, and *Blood: A Scientific Romance* was nominated for a Governor General's Literary Award for Drama. Her work has been presented at the Citadel Theatre, Theatre Calgary, Lunchbox Theatre, the Belfry Theatre, Sage Theatre, Sparrow & Finch Theatre, Theatre Transit, Atomic Vaudeville, and Intrepid Theatre. She is a past member of the Citadel Playwrights Forum and was a playwright-in-residence at Workshop West Playwrights' Theatre. Her next book, *Feminist Resistance: A Graphic Approach* (co-authored with Norah Bowman and Domique Hui), will be published by University of Toronto Press in 2019. Meg currently divides her time between Edmonton as the Lee Playwright in Residence at the University of Alberta and Calgary as the co-director of the Alberta Theatre Projects Playwrights Unit.

First edition: April 2018
Printed and bound in Canada by Imprimerie Gauvin, Gatineau

Jacket design by Kisscut Design
Wallpaper photo © svemar / Shutterstock.com
Tape photo © Picsfive / Shutterstock.com

PLAYWRIGHTS
CANADA PRESS

202-269 Richmond St. W.
Toronto, ON
M5V 1X1

416.703.0013
info@playwrightscanada.com
www.playwrightscanada.com
@playcanpress

MIX
Paper from
responsible sources
FSC® C100212
FSC
www.fsc.org